VOICES OF AGING

VOICES OF AGING

Adult Children and Aging Parents
Talk with God

MISSY BUCHANAN

UPPER ROOM BOOKS®
NASHVILLE

I dedicate this book to the memory of my parents,
Mack and Minelle McGlothlin, who gave my family the greatest gift
that aging parents could ever give their adult children—
compassionate planning for their last season of life
and faith-filled legacies of love.

Upper Room Books® website: books.upperroom.org

UPPER ROOM®, UPPER ROOM BOOKS®, and design logos are trademarks owned by The Upper Room®, a Ministry of GBOD®, Nashville, Tennessee. All rights reserved.

All scripture quotations are from the New Revised Standard Version Bible, copyright © 1989 the Division of Christian Education of the National Council of the Churches of Christ in the United States of America. Used by permission. All rights reserved.

Cover and interior design: Bruce Gore / gorestudio.com
Cover photograph: Oliver Rossi / Getty Images

ISBN 978-0-8358-1366-2 (print)
ISBN 978-0-8358-1367-9 (mobi)
ISBN 978-0-8358-1368-6 (epub)

Printed in the United States of America

CONTENTS

INTRODUCTION

Many would say that I am one of the lucky ones. I was blessed with loving parents who were selfless in preparing for their journeys through aging. I never had to ask them to give up their car keys or have the awkward conversation about moving from their home to an assisted living facility when they no longer could care for themselves. Even as they struggled with physical decline, they valiantly showed the rest of the family how to deal graciously with the heartbreaking loss of independence. Their late lives were far from easy, but their faith remained strong and their actions kind.

I have two siblings who were lovingly involved in the care of our aging parents. Though I was the one who lived closest to our parents and naturally assumed most of the daily caregiving responsibilities, my brother and sister were only a phone call away. They would drop whatever they were doing and make the two-hundred-mile trek to help care for our parents if ever I needed them. I cannot tell you what a comfort that was. They were also mindful of the stress that caregiving put upon my shoulders and thoughtfully offered their support and encouragement in countless other ways.

Still, I know from speaking to many older adults and their families that my family's scenario was more the exception than the rule. As an advocate for seniors and a writer and speaker dealing with issues of aging and faith, I often sit with older adults and hear their frustrations—including those about their grown children. I also talk with adult children who confess the challenges they are facing with their aging loved ones. Even families with strong faith backgrounds and healthy relationships struggle with guilt and stress as they thoughtfully discern the next steps in the journey of aging.

When people ask me for advice, I always suggest that they first try to stand in the shoes of the other generation and look at the situation through that life lens. When practiced intentionally, both older and younger are better equipped to understand and cope with the other's fears and frustrations.

I compiled the scenarios used in this book from conversations I've had with hundreds, even thousands, of aging parents and adult children around the world. As a reader—either an adult child or an older adult—you will likely discover that many of the experiences and feelings expressed in these pages resonate with your own. I present side-by-side the thoughts of younger and older, in both male and female voices, in the hope that you can find yourself in the honest, heartfelt meditations. I invite you to step inside the minds of the two generations and allow your heart to be softened. Ponder the corresponding scripture and be challenged by the action steps of the section *Moving Forward Together*. Conclude with the prayer, either separately or together, and be mindful that each of you speaks to God with the same words. Be in covenant with your loved ones as you journey through aging under the compassionate watch of your Creator.

DOING THE BEST I CAN

Psalm 71:17-18

O God, from my youth you have taught me,
and I still proclaim your wondrous deeds.
So even to old age and gray hairs,
O God, do not forsake me,
until I proclaim your might
to all the generations to come.

Voice of the Adult Child

I wish my mother understood that there are only twenty-four hours
    in my day.
I try to be attentive to her, but she forgets that others need me too.
I have my own family, friends and neighbors, a full-time job
    demanding my time,
church responsibilities, and other commitments.
Every aspect of my life requires a piece of me and my time.
But there's just not enough of me to go around,
not enough time to meet everyone's needs as I would like.
I wish she could understand that I am doing the best I can;
instead, she'd rather try to control me with guilt.
If only I called her more often.
If only I hadn't moved so far away.
If only I cared as much about her as I do about my friends.
If only I were as loyal as so-and-so's daughter.
If only I'd remember how she was there for me when I was a child.
I hear her voice and my own nagging insecurities in my head until I
    feel like a total failure.
I feel obliged to defend myself to her, and I say things I shouldn't.
I know that caring for an aging parent requires sacrificial love,
but I need her to understand that I am trying to do my best
    for everyone.
And in juggling so many responsibilities, I am losing myself.
Help me, Lord.

Voice of the Aging Parent

I hate the thought of becoming a burden on my family members—
of growing frail and struggling in a body debilitated by time
    and disease.
I worry about becoming a drain on their goodwill.
O God, I don't want to complicate their already busy lives or
    deplete their patience.
Still there are moments when I feel like I am alone—
as if I'm the last item on a long to-do list,
as if no one has time for an old person like me.
Lord, forgive me if I become clingy or manipulative in this season
    of vulnerability.
When I feel alone and unwanted, remind me that you will never
    leave my side.
When I am anxious, grant me peace.
When I am disappointed, allow me to encourage others.
O God, help me to remember what it was like when I was younger
    and had countless obligations pressing down.
Close my mouth if I am about to speak a critical word of judgment.
May I live in gratitude for my family's sacrifices and best efforts.
Mold me into a role model for growing old with grace.

Moving Forward Together

Whether you are the aging loved one or the adult child, the journey through aging is often stressful. Learning to maintain balance and reasonable expectations will minimize the strain on everyone involved.

Talk with each other about the frustrations or fears that each generation is experiencing, including feelings of weariness and vulnerability. Try to understand each other's point of view. Work together to define some reasonable expectations. Remember that having a designated day to visit or a regularly scheduled phone call can help calm the anxiety of an older loved one and ease the guilt of an adult child. Creating a rotation system with other family members or friends will also provide a sense of security. Finally, consider how your dependence on others resembles your dependence on God. How can you show God's love by expressing understanding and appreciation for other generations?

Prayer

O Lord of rest and rejuvenation, I am tired of trying to be strong and in control. Help me to remember that you are the fulcrum of a balanced life. Remind me not to judge my own or others' efforts. When I have done my best, let me breathe in your peace and live in grace—not regret. Amen.

CAN'T TAKE IT WITH YOU

Matthew 6:19-21

"Do not store up for yourselves treasures on earth,
where moth and rust consume and where thieves break in and steal;
but store up for yourselves treasures in heaven, where neither moth
nor rust consumes and where thieves do not break in and steal.
For where your treasure is, there your heart will be also."

Voice of the Adult Child

My mind boggles over how much people accumulate in a lifetime.
I look at my mother's overstuffed home
and shudder to think what would happen if she were gone
    tomorrow.
Where would I even begin?
There are things piled high on every shelf and buried deep
    in drawers.
Closets bulge with needless items—
clothing not worn for years, broken appliances, antiques
    collecting dust.
Sometimes I wonder if she ever thinks about how hard it will be for
    her family to deal with all her stuff.
Does she want to leave us the burden of sorting through her
    possessions,
deciding what to keep and what to give away, what has value and
    what doesn't?
If I'm honest with myself I know I'm not so different.
I too have a hard time letting go of my possessions.
I still have awards from middle school and my high school
    yearbooks.
When I want to point a finger of blame, remind me of my own
    tendency to cling to old memories.
How can I help her sort through her past?
What once was manageable—cleaning, throwing away, donating—
    now feels like a daunting task.
Show me how to approach her in a spirit of love and grace.
May I encourage her while also offering compassion.

Voice of the Aging Parent

There are nights when I close my eyes and worry about dying.
Not about whether I'll go to heaven—
about the worn-out underwear in my drawer that my children will
    find after I'm gone.
What will they think as they rummage through the cabinets and
    closets of my life?
Will they snicker about the silly things I've saved over the years—
rusty corncob holders and the tower of empty butter containers in
    the pantry?
Will they heave sighs of relief as they haul trash bags to the curb?
I wish they could understand the differences in our generations.
In my younger days, we scraped and saved to buy every possession.
When something broke, we fixed it. We made do with what we had.
We didn't just toss things out like people do today.
Now I wonder how I can get rid of crafts my children made and
    mementos from long-ago vacations.
O Lord, as I stare into my own mortality, I confess my
    overwhelming fear.
I fear what will be required to get my life in order before I'm gone
    from this earth.
Give me energy to tackle the overflowing closets and the long-
    neglected drawers.
Rid me of the desire to hang onto trivial items.
May I relinquish my pride and invite others to help me discard,
    donate, and organize.
Lighten the heaviness of these moments with sweet remembrances.
Most of all, grant me grace to sort the memories from the mess.

Moving Forward Together

Clutter has a way of constantly nagging at you until you finally decide that enough is enough. No matter your age, you can purge your belongings and lighten your load. Only when you let go can you make room for new growth and fresh possibilities.

Perhaps you feel guilty for even considering parting with items given to you by loved ones. It may help to keep a sampling of your favorite things instead of box loads. Remember that your hope is in God and not in your possessions. If an item has great sentimental value, consider who might benefit most if you gave it away. Use the cleaning-out process as an opportunity to capture the stories of the most cherished items. Record stories about special heirlooms. Take photos of treasured possessions and document their stories in writing. Take courage and begin the process one drawer at a time, one closet at a time.

Prayer

O God, loosen my grip from the stuff that clutters my life. Remind me that I cannot take it with me when I die. Fill me this day with energy and focus to purge that which I no longer need and lighten my load. Removed from the chaos, may I discover the freedom and new possibilities that await. Amen.

THE CAR

2 Corinthians 1:3-4

*Blessed be the God and Father of our Lord Jesus Christ,
the Father of mercies and the God of all consolation, who consoles us
in all our affliction, so that we may be able to console those who
are in any affliction with the consolation with which we
ourselves are consoled by God.*

Voice of the Adult Child

For years I dreaded having the car conversation with my father.

Why can't he understand that I just want him to be safe?

That means giving up the keys to the car before he has a wreck and
    breaks a bone or worse—injures someone else.

Can't he see that he selfishly puts others in danger because of
    his pride?

Lord, I've seen him hit curbs and recklessly turn in front of
    oncoming traffic.

Yet he refuses to admit his reflexes and vision aren't what they used
    to be.

With every attempt to persuade him, he recites the same excuses:

He just drives short distances around town.

*He's a much better driver than teenagers who are busy texting on
    their phones.*

He's still got a driver's license!

How do I reason with someone so stubborn?

How can I explain that it's not all about him?

I've thought about hiding his keys or disabling his car.

I've coaxed and prodded, threatened and ignored, but nothing
    seems to work.

And so I sit and seethe about his obstinate pride and
    irresponsibility.

Help me, Lord.

Voice of the Aging Parent

O Lord, I thought I was prepared for growing older,
but giving up the keys to my car feels like the hardest transition yet.
My family doesn't understand how devastating this will be.
They make it sound as insignificant as giving up my seat on the bus
    to an expectant mother.
But giving up driving means so much more.
Once it is done, my life will never be the same.
I will always be dependent on someone else.
It's just one more reminder of all I've lost in the last few years—
my home, my belongings, my spouse, my health.
Driving remains the last shred of independence I have.
Once I give up the keys, I won't be able to drive to meet friends, to
    church, or to the doctor.
I will become a prisoner in my own home.
I know how the story will likely play out;
I have seen it repeated time and time again with friends.
Family members will make well-intentioned promises
to chauffeur me around wherever I need to go.
But in reality, it won't be long until they become resentful.
They will think that I am imposing on their time—and I suppose I
    will be.
Just once I'd like my children to think about how their lives would
    change if suddenly they couldn't drive.
Help me put aside my frustration, humiliation, and fear.
Dear God, show me what to do.

Moving Forward Together

God understands the fears of both generations when it comes to driving—the threat of injury to older adults or others and the concern of becoming dependent on family members or friends. Ideally, the best time for the car conversation is long before it becomes a critical issue. An older person who proactively designates a trusted person to monitor his driving habits and gives written permission for that person to remove the keys when it become necessary acts unselfishly and thoughtfully.

Before engaging in an awkward conversation about driving, adult children can benefit from an exercise to help better understand an aging parent's fear. For one week, vow not to use your car. Fully experience the frustrations and inconveniences associated with not being able to drive yourself before you approach your aging loved one about giving up the keys. During that time, you might consider alternative transportation such as walking long distances or taking expensive taxi rides, but keep in mind an aging person's physical and financial limitations. In completing the exercise, you will validate the feelings of the older person and will more likely mutually develop a compassionate plan of action that addresses his or her fears.

Prayer

Life changes are not easy, Lord. Giving up the keys to the car feels like one of the most difficult changes of all. Help me to put myself in my loved one's position and experience his or her frustrations and fears. Show me how to find solutions that will honor you in the process. Amen.

WISDOM

Job 12:11-13

"Does not the ear test words
as the palate tastes food?
Is wisdom with the aged,
and understanding in length of days?
With God are wisdom and strength;
he has counsel and understanding."

Voice of the Adult Child

O Lord, I value my mother's stories. Really, I do.
But so much has changed in the last fifty years—
how can I relate to the way things used to be?
The world moves much faster now; our lives are more complicated
    than ever before.
People face more pressure for career success,
more concern about fitness and eating right,
more technologies to learn and engage,
more worries about the economy and healthcare.
How can my mother's experiences be relevant to me now?
Time has marched on and left her behind.
She struggles to use her smartphone; she winces at the computer.
Hot-button news topics leave her bewildered.
She is so out of touch with the realities of modern life.
I confess I tune her out at times.
Forgive me, Lord, when I am dismissive and arrogant.
Humble my heart so that I might discover the wisdom from my
    mother's long life.

Voice of the Aging Parent

My life is a library filled with books that no one reads anymore—
    books of adventure and romance, advice and how-tos.
The books gather dust because no one wants to learn from them.
O Lord, once they were popular volumes, tattered from wear, but
    now no one cares about my life lessons.
As I've grown older, people have less interest in what I have to say
    or what I think.
I have stumbled along my journey, but I can look back across the
    years with wise eyes.
If they were willing, younger folks could learn from my mistakes,
    my follies, my successes.
I have gained knowledge with every experience—
knowledge of broken hearts and unfulfilled dreams,
knowledge of surviving financial woes and raising rebellious teens,
knowledge of eternal truths and the lies of the world.
If only they would ask, I would tell them.

Moving Forward Together

Not everyone grows wise with age. But those who humbly walk with God gain wisdom over time. Wisdom isn't about knowing how to operate the latest piece of technology or keeping up with pop culture. Those with wisdom discern truth and justice in a world filled with many false voices.

As an older person, what might you say to the younger generations that could help them on life's journey? Write a letter. Be vulnerable. Try to move beyond cliché responses and share personal examples of pivotal life lessons you have learned. Refrain from using a lecturing tone. Share the letter with family members and use it as an opportunity for further dialogue. As an adult child, how might you encourage your loved one to share his or her life experiences? How can you affirm the importance of these stories within the context of a swiftly changing world?

Prayer

O Lord, you are the giver of wisdom. Every day I struggle with how to impart my own life lessons and how to learn from others. I ask for your clarity amd guidance. Open my heart and ears. Use my life story to bring fresh insight and understanding to all generations. Amen.

SEASONS

Ecclesiastes 3:1-8

For everything there is a season,
and a time for every matter under heaven:
a time to be born, and a time to die;
a time to plant, and a time to pluck up what is planted;
a time to kill, and a time to heal;
a time to break down, and a time to build up;
a time to weep, and a time to laugh;
a time to mourn, and a time to dance;
a time to throw away stones, and a time to gather stones together;
a time to embrace, and a time to refrain from embracing;
a time to seek, and a time to lose;
a time to keep, and a time to throw away;
a time to tear, and a time to sew;
a time to keep silence, and a time to speak;
a time to love, and a time to hate;
a time for war, and a time for peace.

Voice of the Adult Child

I find myself in the autumn of life, enjoying a comfortable stretch
    of days.
I gather deep thoughts and store up memories for the coming
    winter season.
I've shucked off the heaviest responsibilities of my younger years—
raising children, building careers, planning for financial security.
Now I bask in the light of midlife.
For years I have looked forward to traveling during this season, to
    fulfill long-held dreams to see the world.
But I defer some dreams as I deal with my aging parent's care.
I feel a nagging sensation that winter is not far behind me.
O Lord, I can't help but wonder how long this autumn will last.
I look at my aging loved one and see evidence of what is likely
    to come.
Soon a storm will stir, and the weather will change.
Blustery winds will leave the trees exposed and vulnerable.
I seek understanding for my parent's plight, but I'm not ready to
    prepare for my own winter just yet.
Creator God, let me savor the glories of autumn even as I ponder
    the changing of the seasons that lies ahead.

Voice of the Aging Parent

Time has a way of surprising me.
Just yesterday I was enjoying a delightful autumn—
the trees shone in hues of crimson and gold in the afternoon sun.
But when I lifted my head to enjoy the sun's warmth, autumn
    disappeared and winter arrived.
Now leafless branches cast long shadows onto a frozen landscape,
    creating a scene both solitary and sacred.
I move more slowly now, trudging along, straining to lean into life.
O Lord, I have traveled many miles to reach this season.
In the winter of my life, give me eyes to see the intricate beauty of a
    bare tree silhouetted against a steel-blue sky.
Or the wisdom in wrinkled lines etched upon an aging face.
May I find peace knowing every season contains a rhythm and
    a purpose.
For this day is a gift that I will never have again.
When I start to worry about the winter landscape, remind me that
    underneath the icy ground, new life awaits.

Moving Forward Together

Sometimes you get so focused on the trials in a particular season that you miss the bigger picture of life. Meditate on how God's purpose is unfolding in this season of your life. How do you feel about your current season? How do you relate to the voices of both autumn and winter? Think about ways to celebrate the beauty of your particular season in spite of its challenges. What does it mean to lean into the winter of life with a grateful spirit?

Prayer

O God, I confess that I often lose sight of the beauty in each season of life. I fixate on the uncertainties of tomorrow, and I miss the blessings of today. Melt my frosty heart, Lord. When my life feels barren and lifeless, fill me with your presence. Help me step back and look at life in its fullness. Amen.

MEMORIES

Isaiah 43:18-19

*Do not remember the former things,
or consider the things of old.
I am about to do a new thing;
now it springs forth, do you not perceive it?
I will make a way in the wilderness
and rivers in the desert.*

Voice of the Adult Child

I stare at the pages of a photo album and realize just how much my
    father's life has changed.
The handsome young man in the yellowed photo was athletic
    and energetic.
Not that long ago he lifted me to his shoulders to watch a
    hometown parade.
But now his shoulders are fragile and stooped.
For years I have avoided envisioning him as old, but the signs of
    decline cannot be denied.
O Lord, I must confess I am overwhelmed by grief and
    disappointment.
I feel like I am losing the person I knew as a child—
the one who fixed my bicycle and raced me to the big oak tree in
    the backyard.
That active man has gradually faded into a yellowed photograph,
and I am left to stare into his mortality—and my own.
O God, even as I cherish special memories of long ago,
may I create new memories as we continue on the journey of aging.

Voice of the Aging Parent

It's easy to get stuck in a muddy rut on Memory Lane.

I intend to go for just a short drive but end up lost in the Good
Ol' Days.

Just a glance at an old photo lures me to a time when life seemed
better, easier.

I had more energy and fewer aches and pains.

Life was less complicated and more inviting.

Back in the Good Ol' Days, I felt vibrant, purposeful, needed,
and loved.

But, Lord, I don't want to be that person who lives in the past, who
refuses to budge from how it's always been.

When I feel nostalgiac for life as it once was, steer me back to
the present.

Show me how to visit those long-ago days without getting lost
in time.

If I spend too much time reliving the yesterdays of my life,

I will miss the blessings you give me today.

On this day I will cling to the promise that you will indeed do
something new—something unexpected—in my life

On those days when I glance in the rearview mirror, let me see the
long road of your faithfulness in my life.

Moving Forward Together

Aging is relentless; you cannot deny the signs of aging all around you. Adult children often have difficulty acknowledging the changes in older loved ones because those changes bring them face-to-face with their own mortality. Aging parents often seek comfort in reminiscing about days past. Those connections to days gone by provide a grounding experience, especially as the world seems to be speeding up and moving past them.

What tempts you to dwell too long in the past? How might living in the past keep you from leaving the legacy you want? Today, take one action that will create a positive new memory for you and your loved one.

Prayer

O God, I am tempted to settle in the past and stay there. Often I dig my heels deep into the mud of the past and resist moving forward. Teach me how to visit the past without dwelling there. Help me come to terms with my mortality. Show me how to continue on this journey of aging, Lord, knowing that you always are doing a new thing in my life. Amen.

DOCTORS AND HOSPITALS

1 Corinthians 6:19-20

Do you not know that your body is a temple of the Holy Spirit within you, which you have from God, and that you are not your own? For you were bought with a price; therefore glorify God in your body.

Voice of the Adult Child

Every week my mother has another doctor's appointment,
another medical test, another reason for me to take off work and
     rearrange my schedule.
Once I could drop her off or sit in the waiting room until she
     finished.
Now she needs me in the exam room as her advocate, an extra set
     of ears to interpret medical terms and treatment plans.
We always encounter new forms to complete—
emergency contacts, insurance information, dates of ailments and
     surgeries from long ago,
endless questions about prescriptions, allergies, family history,
     and immunizations.
I spend time every week helping her navigate the medical maze.
Lord, I feel overwhelmed and frustrated.
 I look into her face and see her own sorrows and fears.
As I struggle with impatience, dear God, whisper your peace into
     my soul so that I may offer comfort to her.

Voice of the Aging Parent

I used to go to the doctor for an occasional checkup or to get my
flu shot.
I dashed through the usual battery of tests with little thought
or concern.
But now that I am older, doctor visits are no longer simple
or routine.
My life feels like an unending string of medical visits full of poking
and prodding.
An ophthalmologist, a rheumatologist, a colonoscopy, an EKG.
At every appointment, I face a new round of questions.
It's little wonder my blood pressure is high.
O Lord, before these weary bones can even crawl up on the exam
table, I am exhausted.
Then I have to strain to understand what the doctor is saying.
I am so grateful that my daughter can accompany me on these
appointments, but I feel guilty for taking up her time.
When I begin to feel betrayed by this old body, Lord, help me to
remember its beautiful and intricate design.
May I care for it as best I can for as long as I can.

Moving Forward Together

Older adults often list dealing with chronic health issues as one of the most difficult aspects of aging. Tiring walks through medical buildings, uncomfortable procedures, finding the right medications, and worrying about diagnoses all stir up uncertainty and stress. Add to that a loss of vision and hearing—it's not surprising most older adults see medical appointments as mixed blessings. As difficult as it may seem, medical appointments can provide opportunities to discuss important end-of-life decisions.

Reflect on ways that medical visits might be less stressful for both generations. How might standing in the shoes of the older person help a younger person to plan differently for outings to the doctor? Consider what it means to glorify God *in* your body, even when your body is wearing out.

Prayer

O God, I confess that I complain and easily forget that my body is your amazing design. Every seemingly simple bodily act arises out of interconnected, complex functions conceived by you. You created the laws of nature that change my body over time. Enable me to accept my reality and celebrate the marvelous intricacy of your creation. Amen.

PARENT/CHILD

1 Peter 5:3-6

*Do not lord it over those in your charge, but be examples to the flock.
And when the chief shepherd appears, you will win the crown of glory
that never fades away. In the same way, you who are younger must
accept the authority of the elders. And all of you must clothe yourselves
with humility in your dealings with one another, for
"God opposes the proud,
but gives grace to the humble."
Humble yourselves therefore under the mighty hand of God, so that
he may exalt you in due time.*

Voice of the Adult Child

Will she ever realize that I'm no longer a child?

For heaven's sake, I've been an adult for decades— an adult with a
     college degree, a successful career, a family of my own.

So why does my mother still treat me as if I'm five years old?

I'm able to make my own decisions and care for myself.

Don't leave without your umbrella. It might rain today.

I can't believe you paid so much for that!

The grass is getting high. Is your lawn mower broken?

I suppose she thinks she's helping with her less-than-subtle
     remarks.

In truth, her comments drone on like a dripping faucet that erodes
     my patience until it finally creates a hole in my heart.

O Lord, I confess that sometimes I react like a defensive teen.

I roll my eyes and respond with careless, sarcastic remarks.

And even when I manage to stay silent, surely my thoughts are
     written on my face.

That's when a wave of guilt sweeps over me, knocking me to
     my knees.

Honor your father and mother—the command echoes in my mind.

But how do I show honor when my parent doesn't respect me as
     an adult?

O Lord, I tire of shouldering this heavy bag of mixed-up feelings—
     frustration, guilt, embarrassment, sorrow, love, and anger.

When pride keeps me from reaching out to my mother, soften
     my heart.

God, grant me wisdom and grace to be the adult child you call me
     to be.

Voice of the Aging Parent

Sometimes I feel obsolete. Unnecessary. Irrelevant.
Like a carton of milk whose expiration date is long past.
Some days I feel soured by circumstances out of my control—
times when the schism between my generation and the next leaves
    me feeling stupid and out of touch.
O God, growing old makes me unsettled and takes me away from
    the familiar.
Once I had a career, a family to raise, a home to maintain.
But now it feels as though my work is done.
My purpose is little more than a vapor—a thin, elusive trail of
    smoke that quickly vanishes into nothingness.
Lord, is it wrong that I still yearn to be needed?
To know that I matter to someone? To know others value my
    life lessons?
I bristle when younger people talk to me as if I am a child.
How easily they forget that my life experiences far outnumber
    theirs.
Still I confess sometimes I impose my advice with little regard for
    their feelings.
Forgive me, Lord. Remove the self-pity from my heart.
When I feel left out because I can't keep up with the pace of change,
    may I take refuge in your steadfast love.
Remind me that you give me purpose as long as I have breath.
Show me how to use these late years to influence others without
    lecture or judgmental comments.
Flood my heart with grace so that I become an example to others of
    how to age well.

Moving Forward Together

It takes humility before God to build and maintain healthy relation-ships at any age. If you seek first to understand another person, you are more likely to be understood. Make an effort to put yourself in the place of someone in a different generation and humbly ask God to give you new insight. Then as you and your loved one journey together, keep in mind an important rule for nurturing your relation-ship: Compliment each other openly and often; confront privately and infrequently. Now make a list of ten characteristics you most admire about your older or younger loved one. Share the lists with each other.

Prayer

O Lord, the landscape of aging looks uneven and daunting at times. I often lose my footing. Help me cling to you through the frustrations and uncertainty of life. Steady me and give me grace enough to offer others respect and honor. Amen.

MONEY

1 Timothy 6:10

The love of money is a root of all kinds of evil, and in their eagerness to be rich some have wandered away from the faith and pierced themselves with many pains.

Voice of the Adult Child

Money—it's never far from my mind.

At my age, I often think about my retirement and saving accounts.

How long will I need to work? How much can I spend?

And now I worry about my father's money too.

In the past he was mentally sharp, able to manage his own finances.

But now he struggles with simple mathematics and paying his bills
on time.

Managing money has become a burden that is too weighty for his
aging mind, but he's not ready to relinquish control.

Just talking about money makes him uneasy.

He worries about privacy and independence.

I worry about him running out of funds or being manipulated by
greedy family members or financial scams.

His uncertain future complicates his financial state.

Will he require professional caregivers?

What if he suffers a medical crisis that insurance won't cover?

What if he naively drains his financial resources and becomes
dependent on the family?

I confess a troubled spirit, Lord. I don't know what to do.

Voice of the Aging Parent

Uncertainty is stressful, especially when it comes to money.
Some days I'd like to know how much longer I'll live so I can ration
    my money appropriately.
Money affects so many decisions about my life:
where I'll live, what I'll eat, where I'll go, what I can give away.
Managing money is a daunting task, but I'm not ready to
    relinquish control.
I hate to admit it, but I have concerns about a few family members
    who seem more interested in my finances than my well-being.
I wish I could see behind their smiles to the very core of
    their intentions.
Perhaps my family thinks I'm stingy or naive.
In reality, I am afraid—afraid of losing control, afraid of outliving
    my resources.
My mind is scrambled by interest rates and stock-market trends.
O Lord, I can no longer trust myself to manage my money, but I'm
    unsure what to do.
Help me to be financially wise.

Moving Forward Together

As scripture tells us, money is not a root of evil—the *love* of money is. This topic definitely stirs up a lot of emotion in family members. For some, the staggering cost of caregiving and health care are central issues. For others, conversation centers around who will be responsible for financial oversight once an older adult can no longer manage his or her finances. Some older adults have ample financial resources but refuse to spend money on needed assistance for fear of diminishing the inheritance they want to leave family members.

As an aging parent, make a conscious effort to discuss financial matters with someone you trust. Have financial issues become burdensome? If so, how? What obstacles are you experiencing in regard to financial matters? As an adult child, think of important questions you need to ask your aging parent about financial matters as they relate to his or her well-being. Consider together how you both might be crowding God out of important decisions. In what ways can your situation be improved?

Prayer

Lord, I am walking on shaky financial ground. Money worries cause me stress and pain. I surrender my concerns to you. I commit to seeking your wisdom in the uncertainty of the future. Amen.

DIGNITY

John 13:34-35

"I give you a new commandment, that you love one another. Just as I have loved you, you also should love one another. By this everyone will know that you are my disciples, if you have love for one another."

Voice of the Adult Child

When it comes to my aging parent,
I find it difficult to straddle the line between her need for
   independence and her need for assistance.
How can I be supportive of her desire to be on her own without
   neglecting her safety and dignity?
There are times when she doesn't notice spills and odors,
when I must protect her from herself,
when I overrule what she wants for her own best interest.
O Lord, I confess that I get frustrated and treat her like a child.
Forgive me.
I feel the tension between preserving her self-esteem and
   maintaining my sanity.
My heart breaks for the once independent woman who is losing
   her abilities.
She cannot always see what I see or hear what I hear.
But in my efforts to help her, I am not always mindful of her
   privacy and dignity.
Help me to be sensitive to her situation—to her fear, her
   embarrassment.
May I offer her dignity as best I can, knowing that growing older is
   not easy.

Voice of the Aging Parent

I remember sitting in my room while my children talked about me
    as if I weren't even there.
They spoke as though I didn't hear or understand their words.
Maybe they think they have the right to make decisions about
    my life.
They don't seem to understand that even though I am growing
    older, it is still my life. *My life.*
I realize I cannot do many of the things I once did, but I am still me
    inside this old body.
I have feelings like anyone else, and I desperately need my dignity.
It's hard enough that old age assaults my independence
    and privacy;
I have to depend on others to help with the most intimate parts of
    my life.
But it's made worse when I'm treated like an infant.
Forgive me when I become embarrassed and stiffen my spine in
    stubborn pride.
O God, you know the longings of my heart.
Show me how to graciously accept help knowing that you have
    given me dignity, no matter my circumstances.

Moving Forward Together

No matter your age, you yearn for dignity. Your self-esteem takes a beating as you grow older and require more help. Think of a few examples of how an older person's dignity can be protected as he or she ages. How can fulfilling God's commandment to love one another change the dynamics in your current situation? In what ways can you nurture an adult-to-adult relationship even as one is growing frail?

Prayer

Like the air I breathe, dignity is essential to my living, Lord. You have made me in your image and given me worth. Forgive me when I fail to respect others. Help me to diligently guard against words and deeds that strip away the dignity of those I encounter. Amen.

HOME

Joshua 1:9

*"I hereby command you: Be strong and courageous; do not be frightened or dismayed, for the L*ORD *your God is with you wherever you go."*

Voice of the Adult Child

My dad is standing on the front porch looking out across an
    overgrown flowerbed.
Weeds have overtaken the beds, and the blooms have long
    since withered.
Once his yard was well-manicured, a source of pride.
But not now.
Inside the house I see more signs of neglect—
a refrigerator stuffed with moldy leftovers, piles of mail and papers,
    dirty clothes hanging on doorknobs.
I look around and my throat tightens as I contemplate the future.
No one wants to be told it's time to move out of his own home.
But he can't stay alone in this house any longer.
It's too much, Lord. Too much for one person at this stage of life.
Can't he see there's no shame in admitting that he just can't do
    it anymore?
Why does he demand to live the rest of his days in this house when
    it's no longer safe?
I want him to be able to stay, but it's just not practical.
And so I will end up being the villain—the one who finally forces
    this vulnerable man to concede.
O Lord, how do I help him understand how painful this is for
    me too?
I pray that he will discover the blessings of a new home—friends,
    meaningful activities, and community.
May he embrace new experiences in the midst of saying good-bye.

Voice of the Aging Parent

_____

I gaze out the window at the oak tree my children and
    grandchildren used to climb.
Now that I am alone, the memories of this house comfort me.
I wish I could roll back the clock to an earlier time when laughter
    and music filled these rooms, but I can't.
On days when I feel sad and lonely, I find comfort in the familiarity
    of home. *My home.*
The kitchen window overlooks the crape myrtle that blooms
    every spring.
The squeaky screen door announces a neighbor's arrival.
The workshop smells of oil and wood shavings.
My family members think it is time for me to move, but I cannot
    imagine my life compressed into a single-room apartment.
I have tried to digest their concerns—
I need more help; I can no longer live safely on my own; I am alone;
    my home is too expensive to maintain.
I know they mean well, but the idea of moving brings anxiety
    and fear.
O Lord, I don't know what to do.
How can I leave the place that brings so much joy to what time I
    have left?
Comfort me, God, and give me direction.

Moving Forward Together

Adult children often underestimate the emotional turmoil for an aging person of moving away from a beloved home. Home represents all that is familiar. It provides a sense of comfort, privacy, and independence. The thought of losing these things can be overwhelming. But for many older adults, a time will come when a move is necessary for safety or financial reasons.

As an older adult, review your own situation. Gently peel back the emotional layers to learn what fears and concerns lie at your core. In what ways might those fears be addressed? Are you holding to God's promise, or are you clinging to the past? How can trusting God's promise to be with you wherever you go change your outlook? Meditate on the idea that God might want to take you to a situation that is better than what you are clinging to right now. Could God be inviting you to embrace a change? How might you help recreate a sense of home in a new place?

As an adult child, consider ways you can bring a sense of home to an aging parent's new residence. Ask him or her what personal items hold special significance. Find new ways to display those treasures. Create a wall of favorite photographs, and talk about each one as you hang it. Make a scrapbook with photos of meaningful belongings that he or she is unable to bring to the senior residence.

Prayer

Remind me, O Lord, that wherever I go, you will always be there. Prompt me to lean forward into new life experiences with a positive attitude. Enable me to help others in difficult life transitions and to remember that in eternity there will be no more good-byes. Amen.

SIBLINGS

Romans 12:10-14

Love one another with mutual affection; outdo one another in showing honor. Do not lag in zeal, be ardent in spirit, serve the Lord. Rejoice in hope, be patient in suffering, persevere in prayer. Contribute to the needs of the saints; extend hospitality to strangers. Bless those who persecute you; bless and do not curse them.

Voice of the Adult Child

I just ran into a brick wall. Again.

My brother refuses to help care for our aging mother.

Though he lives only a few miles from our mother, he can recite a
catalog of excuses for why he doesn't visit.

He's too busy with work. His kids need him. Visiting our mother is
too emotionally draining.

He only calls when I beg him or when he wants something
from her.

How can he drive by her neighborhood and not stop in for a
few minutes?

For heaven's sake, he has a responsibility to help care for his
own mother!

And so from hundreds of miles away, I carry the burden of our
mother's care.

I make the trek every few weeks to clean her house and pay the bills
while he takes the easy way out.

He says I'm so much better at dealing with our mother than he is.

O Lord, how can I show love and grace to someone who shirks his
family responsibilities?

At times the strain is more than I can bear, especially when he
criticizes me or hints about receiving an early inheritance.

To make matters worse, our mother makes excuses for him.

Dear God, I love my mother, but I have my own family laden
with responsibilities.

I feel furious. Frustrated. Hurt. Overwhelmed. Weary. Desperate.

Help me, Lord.

Voice of the Aging Parent

I never wanted this to happen.
In my old age, I am the reason for a rift between my children.
I suppose there has always been an undercurrent of sibling
    discontent, but I never thought it would come to this.
Now they argue about what they are going to do with me, about
    whose turn it is to care for me.
My daughter is fatigued; I can see it in her tightly pinched face.
When she talks about her brother, there's anger in her voice.
On rare occasions when my son visits, he squirms nervously as if he
    can't wait to leave.
I hear him grumble about his sister under his breath.
Their disharmony is breaking my heart and my spirit, Lord.
It's all because of me, and I don't know what to do.
I never wanted to be the old person that others dreaded to visit.
I never wanted to be the one who caused problems for her children.
My heart swells with gratitude when I think about the sacrifices my
    daughter has made to care for me.
I can't imagine what I'd do without her, but does she really expect
    me to turn my back on my own son?
So I pretend that all is well when deep down I know it's not.
Help me, Lord.

Moving Forward Together

Family dynamics can prove complicated, especially when discussing the care of an aging parent. How have you and your family members organized caregiving responsibilities around God's command to love one another? Are caregiving roles disproportionate in your family situation? Are you trying to escape the hardships involved in caring for an aging loved one? Do you feel that a family member imposes undue responsibility or guilt onto another family member? How might discrepancies in geographical distance be lovingly addressed within your family?

With the scripture verse in mind, determine how family members can be truly devoted to one another. Ask God to reveal a way to redefine caregiving tasks so that your family will honor God by utilizing your different gifts, time constraints, and abilities.

Prayer

I confess that my family squabbles are hurting everyone. How can I work with my family members in the midst of a fight? Forgive me, Lord. Turn my excuses into acts of compassion and my resentments into heartfelt appreciation for others. If I am serving you first, O God, I will find harmony on the journey. Amen.

STRESS

Romans 5:3-5

Not only that, but we also boast in our sufferings, knowing that suffering produces endurance, and endurance produces character, and character produces hope, and hope does not disappoint us, because God's love has been poured into our hearts through the Holy Spirit that has been given to us.

Voice of the Adult Child

After visiting my father today, I went to the car, lay my head on the
steering wheel, and cried like a two-year-old child.

Ugly tears, a contorted face, and red nose.

O Lord, I'm burned out. Frazzled. I don't even recognize myself
anymore.

Today the stress just spilled out when my father complained that I
bought him the wrong brand of paper towels.

I felt my blood pressure shoot up like a candy thermometer thrust
into boiling water.

What about the times I raced him to the emergency room?

What about the doctor visits and grocery store runs?

I've cut hundreds of pills in half and organized them in daily
containers.

I've cooked countless meals and put them in his freezer.

I've purged his belongings, packed up his life, and moved him to a
senior community.

While squeezing in time to visit him, I have been squeezing out the
joy in my own life.

There are days when he doesn't seem to appreciate my efforts, Lord.

Days when my soup is too thick or the chicken too dry.

Other times, he seems so helpless and vulnerable.

I can't help but feel compassion toward him.

O God, there seems to be no light at the end of the tunnel.

Give me hope, Lord.

Voice of the Aging Parent

Even before I close my eyes at night, my mind starts to spin
    with questions.
What if my family moves me from this apartment to a
    nursing home?
What if I fall and no one finds me?
What if I get dementia? Who will care for me?
What if I receive bad news from the doctor?
What if my medications become too expensive for me to afford?
Then there are concerns about incontinence. Money. Loneliness.
I let my imagination run wild until I've worked myself into a frenzy.
To an outsider, my life probably seems routine—even boring.
I spend most of my time in my favorite recliner watching television.
My life appears carefree.
But underneath the relaxed facade rages a maelstrom of worry.
O Lord, I am so frustrated by all the things I can no longer do.
When surrounded by my family, I try to act as though I have it all
    under control.
I know they are always checking up on me—
listening for evidence that my memory is slipping,
looking at my clothes to make sure they are clean, buttoned,
    and zippered.
They already do so much for me.
I am afraid to let them know just how much I depend on them.
I feel captive in my own deteriorating body.
O Lord, save me from myself.

Moving Forward Together

Life transitions bring change, and change fuels stress. Think about how the stress of your current situation has impacted your relationship with God. Do you call out to God only in moments of crisis, or have you developed a daily spiritual practice of prayer? Developing prayer as a spiritual practice will better prepare you to deal with the stress that naturally comes with caregiving and aging. Regular conversation with God provides an opportunity to safely vent frustrations. Focusing on God's strength instead of your own can also help you stop trying to control things that are out of your control.

Recall a stressful time in the past when you felt the hand of God move in your life. Consider how you can draw on that experience now. As you read the voice of each generation, try to stand in the shoes of the other person in order to better understand his or her feelings. Never forget God's gift of tears. Sometimes it's beneficial to have a good cry and let God redeem the pain.

Prayer

Dear Lord, give me eyes to see beyond the stress of my situation. May I not lose sight of the most important part of any relationship: love. Help me look beyond my frustration and fear to your boundless grace. In the mess of life, guide me to act with kindness and gratitude. Amen.

FRIENDS

Mark 2:2-5

So many gathered around that there was no longer room for them, not even in front of the door; and [Jesus] was speaking the word to them. Then some people came, bringing to him a paralyzed man, carried by four of them. And when they could not bring him to Jesus because of the crowd, they removed the roof above him; and after having dug through it, they let down the mat on which the paralytic lay. When Jesus saw their faith, he said to the paralytic, "Son, your sins are forgiven."

Voice of the Adult Child

Through the struggles of caregiving, I have discovered who my real
 friends are.
They are the ones who have been there for me, serving as
 cheerleaders, therapists, and errand-runners.
On difficult days, they let me vent my frustrations without thinking
 I'm a bad person.
My friends make time for me even when I can't seem to make time
 for them.
They help me face my problems head-on but never lecture me.
They encourage me but never try to change me into someone else.
They offer no righteous indignation—only love and grace.
Through this journey with my aging parent, I have learned that real
 friends don't drift away like unmoored boats in a storm.
When I am hanging by a thread, they anchor me, strengthen me,
 and make me laugh when I'm too tired to think.
For this gift of friendship, I am eternally grateful.
Thank you, Lord, for the healing salve of friendship for my
 stressed-out heart.

Voice of the Aging Parent

Sometimes I play a game in my mind—
a somber game older folks secretly play but don't talk about much.
It's the *Who Will Be Next?* game.
I am losing my friends one by one.
Some have moved away. Others have died.
I'm left to wonder who will be next.
My closest friend moved to be near her family in a faraway state.
Longtime church friends became ill and died.
Others left for senior care centers across town.
My circle of friends is shrinking, Lord.
I am left with their empty seats in the dining hall and gaping holes
    in my heart.
I don't think my family understands how much I miss my friends.
I look through stacks of old photographs and celebrate
    the memories.
But there are dark days when I feel alone.
O Lord, I need friends to come alongside me on this journey.
I need to hear their laughter and feel their warm embrace.
I need friends who will cheer me up when I am feeling down.
Friends who will encourage me to keep moving when I want to sit
    down and quit.
Hear my groaning, Lord, and draw me close.
For I have not outgrown my need for friends.

Moving Forward Together

Never underestimate the importance of friendship in any stage of life. People without a strong network of friends are more likely to feel isolated, lonely, and depressed. Caregivers also need the support of close friends for their own encouragement and to help them navigate stressful times.

Revisit the story of the paralytic and his friends who carried him to where Jesus was preaching. They dug a hole in the roof so they could lower their friend down to see Jesus face-to-face. How does that story of friendship encourage or challenge you today? Meditate on the importance of friendship and faith in the scripture, then apply it to your life. What practical steps can younger persons take to create opportunities for older loved ones to reconnect with friends? In what ways might older loved ones be encouraged to build new friendships? How can older loved ones show support for their adult children who need to nurture their own friendships?

Prayer

Dear Lord, you know my needs so well. You have sent friends into my life to share my joy, to make me laugh, and to ache and weep with me when I hurt. Theirs is the gift of presence. As I age, show me how to treasure and nurture these friendships. Then open my eyes to opportunities to make new friends as well. Amen.

HOLIDAYS

Ecclesiastes 3:12-14

I know that there is nothing better for them than to be happy and enjoy themselves as long as they live; moreover, it is God's gift that all should eat and drink and take pleasure in all their toil. I know that whatever God does endures forever; nothing can be added to it, nor anything taken from it; God has done this, so that all should stand in awe before him.

Voice of the Adult Child

Maybe it's silly, but I fantasize about picture-perfect holidays.
The kind where the family gathers around the Christmas tree,
watches fireworks together on a summer night,
shares laughter and good food, makes memories.
And so I decorate with Easter bunnies, patriotic flags, scarecrows,
    and nativity scenes—each for its appropriate season.
Now that my children are grown and scattered with families of
    their own,
holidays keep us connected, and that's more important to me
    than ever.
Why then do I dread them so?
O Lord, trying to balance the desires of my mother with the needs
    of younger family members is getting more difficult.
I wish my mother could see how hard I'm trying to make the
    holidays special.
She gets irritable with the commotion that naturally comes with a
    large family.
She complains about how late we eat and how the teenagers never
    look up from their cell phones.
I wish I knew how to satisfy her.
The pressure of creating a memorable holiday takes its toll on
    my patience.
I want to enjoy the holidays with those I love instead of dread them.

Voice of the Aging Parent

There was a time when I fussed over every holiday, trying to create
  special memories for family and friends.
I cleaned and baked, decorated and shopped.
But now that I've grown older, I haven't the energy to celebrate in a
  big way.
O God, at my age the holidays just stir up confusing feelings.
I feel joy laced with sadness, excitement mixed with dread, sweet
  memories mingled with devastating grief.
I look forward to having family and friends gathered around,
but there's also an empty chair where my husband used to sit.
At times the laughter and conversation sounds like chaos to me—
everyone talking at once, children running around, toys scattered
  like an obstacle course.
My family forgets that I can't hear what is being said.
That I am afraid of falling.
That I don't have the energy I once did.
They probably think I'm being cantankerous.
But even in a house full of family and friends, I somehow feel alone.

Moving Forward Together

In an effort to create a picture-perfect celebration, it's easy to miss the voice of God reminding you that holiday perfection is only an illusion. Even with the commotion that comes with multiple generations being under one roof, you have the opportunity to create harmony and wonderful memories. But first you must set aside the notion of perfection and focus instead on strengthening relationships and making memories together.

Try to understand the limitations and frustrations of an older person for whom holidays are both a source of joy and worry. How might holiday plans be altered so that safety and comfort become priorities? Instead of staying for an all-day affair, maybe an older person would be more content with just a few hours. Think about how the whole family could show more sensitivity to another's hearing or vision impairment. How can you help an older person feel more a part of the festivities? Ask an older loved one to offer the family blessing or tell a favorite holiday story from years past. In what ways could the entire family pay a joyful tribute to those who have passed on? While honoring long-held traditions, how might you create space for new memories?

Prayer

O Lord, I yearn for a Norman Rockwell holiday—joyous, memorable, and harmonious. But in seeking perfection, I forget to seek you. Show me how to merge the generations in celebration, love, and acts of kindness to one another. Calm me when my frustrations flare. Let me experience your peace as I celebrate the gift of family. Amen.

BOUNDARIES

Mark 6:45-46

Immediately [Jesus] made his disciples get into the boat and go on ahead to the other side, to Bethsaida, while he dismissed the crowd. After saying farewell to them, he went up on the mountain to pray.

Voice of the Adult Child

Saying no may be the hardest thing I do, especially when it comes
    to my aging parent.
I've tried so hard to fulfill his expectations, but I must draw the line
    before I collapse in exhaustion and frustration.
I know in my head that boundaries are important, but my heart is
    lagging behind.
Why do I still feel the need to please him?
I feel guilty, as though I'm not doing enough.
As though I am turning my back on my father.
And on you, God.
Over the years his needs have increased, but my time and energy
    have not.
There are times when I knowingly allow him to take advantage of
    my goodwill because it's easier to say yes than to explain a no.
I take his criticism personally, and I get angry with myself.
I care deeply about him even when we don't see eye to eye about
    what is best.
O Lord, I have no superpowers.
I need help in this ever-changing relationship with my
    aging parent.
It is easier to set boundaries than to keep them.
Give me courage to turn my good intentions into acts of wisdom.

Voice of the Aging Parent

Growing older is like making your way up a mountain on a narrow
 dirt road.
There are no guardrails or road signs to warn you of the
 danger ahead.
Sharp hairpin curves with steep drop-offs on both sides
 appear unexpectedly.
O God, sometimes the uncertainty of aging makes me sick
 with anxiety.
At this stage of life I have to depend on other people to care for me.
It's both humiliating and frustrating.
Still I confess that too often I have acted more like a bossy child
 than a grateful parent.
I fail to thank family members for all they have done for me.
Forgive me, Lord, when I overinflate my parental role and try to
 direct their lives.
I know we're all trying to navigate our way through constant change,
but help my family members understand that I have boundaries too.
Lord, please open our eyes to ways that we unintentionally hurt
 each other.
Help me to show the appreciation and affirmation that I hold in
 my heart.

Moving Forward Together

Setting boundaries is a loving way to establish and meet reasonable expectations between adult children and aging parents, especially when circumstances constantly change. Scripture affirms that Jesus knew the importance of boundaries. Although loving and kind, he didn't always do what others asked of him. At times he withdrew from the crowds for rest and prayer. He also refused to be manipulated by others, including religious leaders.

What kind of inner battles are you experiencing regarding your loved one? What boundaries are necessary to protect your well-being? Consider how Jesus provides a model for you. Choose a time and place to have an unhurried, private conversation with your loved one regarding your expectations and your boundaries.

Begin by affirming how stressful and frustrating this life transition must be for the other person and demonstrate that you are trying to understand his or her perspective. Explain to each other why your personal limits are important. Be careful not to blame. Share thoughts about how best to deal with each other's expectations. Be clear about your boundaries; be kind but consistent if disagreements occur in the future.

Prayer

Dear Lord, aging is difficult in ways I cannot always foresee. I stumble over my own expectations. I fall to the ground, weary and worn. Help me depend on you to guide my way. Teach me how to honor my loved one's boundaries—and my own. Amen.

DEATH

Romans 14:7-8

We do not live to ourselves, and we do not die to ourselves. If we live, we live to the Lord, and if we die, we die to the Lord; so then, whether we live or whether we die, we are the Lord's.

Voice of the Adult Child

I don't like to think about death.

Images of stone-cold bodies appear in my mind and linger long
     after funerals are over.

Why should I deliberately ponder something so upsetting?

So I shy away from conversations about death and dying and focus
     on staying young for as long as I can.

Exercise and a healthy diet. Fish oil, blueberries, and omega-3s.

O Lord, I know I'm going to die at some point, but I don't need to
     be reminded every day.

Still there are times when I cannot get death out of my mind.

Especially now that I am caring for my aging loved one,

I am forced to think about death in ways I'd rather not.

Hospice care and living wills. Do Not Resuscitate forms. Cremation
     or casket?

These words are casually tossed around with little regard to their
     harsh finality.

Dear God, you know I am struggling with the hard facts of death.

When I think of my father, I can't imagine life without him.

Give me confidence to accept that embracing death will help me
     understand life.

Voice of the Aging Parent

I am not afraid of dying—it's not knowing how life will unfold
    between now and then that concerns me most.
Sometimes I wonder if I will linger for months, even years, as a
    flickering candle.
Or will I simply be snuffed out with a single gust?
Will I be in my own bed surrounded by family?
In a hospital room or nursing home?
Will death come unexpectedly in my sleep, or will I have warning
    that the end is very near?
I know this for certain: Death will come.
It cannot be stopped.
But every time I try to talk about it with my son, he throws his
    hands up like a traffic cop and sputters,
"Not now. We're not going to talk about it."
He doesn't understand that I need to talk about it.
I am not afraid to talk about it.
Death will come, and my unfulfilled dreams will be buried
    alongside me.
But death won't be the end of my story; it will be a new beginning.
As I learn to accept the reality of death, help me to embrace life
    more fully.

Moving Forward Together

You must not blind your eyes to tough realities of aging or pretend that you can somehow avoid death if you work hard enough. Over and over in scripture, God sends messengers to tell others not to be afraid. As a believer, you must learn to accept your own mortality. Are you afraid to have conversations about death? How can having those difficult conversations serve as a gift to you and your loved one?

Think about how contemplating death can help you use your time more wisely today. How can you look forward to the new things that God will do in the future while also remaining realistic about death?

Prayer

Dear Lord, use my conversations with my loved one about dying and death to bring new insight into what it means to live fully in you. Help me release my grip on worldly things so that I can grasp eternity. Keep me spiritually alive until I take my last breath. Amen.

LAUGHTER

Proverbs 17:22

A cheerful heart is a good medicine,
but a downcast spirit dries up the bones.

Voice of the Adult Child

Just when I feel as though I am going to lose my mind,
my father says something so ridiculously funny that I burst
     out laughing.
He always catches me by surprise.
He doesn't even realize that he is being funny.
Suddenly something hysterical comes out of his mouth, and my
     mood lifts in that single moment.
O God, thank you for the gift of laughter.
I desperately need those moments that turn somber events into
     funny ones, moments that change dread to joy.
On those dark days, I need to throw back my head and let the air
     fill my lungs.
Not the kind of laughter that hurts other people but the kind that
     heals and replenishes wilted spirits.
O Lord, when life is drilling down on me, give me a big dose
     of laughter—
hearty laughter that lightens my mood and gives me hope again.

Voice of the Aging Parent

When I look into the mirror, I figure I can either laugh or cry.

I see a droopy body and a face that resembles a wrinkled, old dog.

Without much effort, I could get depressed at the sight.

O Lord, sometimes life gets so serious that I just need to laugh.

So I look for the humor in old age and laugh at my circumstances
    as best I can.

Just this morning I felt like an unhinged screen door blowing in the
    breeze as I tried to get out of my chair.

I rocked back and forth five times before I finally made it my feet.

Yesterday I laughed out loud when I couldn't even open the packet
    of honey to spread on my biscuit.

There are times when I step out into the sunlight and notice that
    I'm wearing socks that don't match.

Or that I've buttoned my shirt wrong.

Growing old is tough, God, but I know it doesn't help to get upset.

If I take my predicament too seriously, I will likely become sad.

So until my last breath, I hope to laugh.

Moving Forward Together

Laughter is one of God's greatest gifts. It relieves stress and brings a fresh perspective on any situation. So it's time to get serious about laughing!

Think about how you might be more intentionally playful in times of stress and frustration. What funny stories can you share from the past or from your daily life? What jokes or cartoons could you share with others to lighten the mood? Surround yourself with people who make you laugh. Then remember that it is better to age with laughter than to grow old in misery.

Prayer

O God, I thank you for the freeing gift of laughter, especially when daily life wears me down. If life begins to drain my good spirits, attune my ears to the laughter of children and the jokes of friends. Delight me in the most unlikely circumstances! Turn my earthly frustrations into the heavenly sounds of laughter. Amen.

OFF-CENTER

Ephesians 2:7-10

So that in the ages to come [God] might show the immeasurable riches of his grace in kindness toward us in Christ Jesus. For by grace you have been saved through faith, and this is not your own doing; it is the gift of God—not the result of works, so that no one may boast. For we are what he has made us, created in Christ Jesus for good works, which God prepared beforehand to be our way of life.

Voice of the Adult Child

Some days I feel lopsided—
a lump of clay thrown off-center onto the potter's wheel.
Wobbling from side to side in a world that is spinning too fast.
There are times when nothing seems to work out quite right no
     matter how hard I try.
The clay is too dry. Too wet. Too lumpy.
I run frantically from task to task but never complete any of them.
In a moment of frustration, I say something thoughtless and hurt
     my older loved one.
I complain to others. I blame. I obsess.
I spin too fast until life finally collapses in on me.
Forgive me when I flounder, Lord.
I want to be pliable. Adaptable. Ready to embrace life transitions.
Help me to find my center again.
When caregiving takes a toll on my health and emotional resources,
     recenter me.
You alone bring balance to my life, Lord.
It is only when I willingly lay my life on your potter's wheel that
     you can mold me into the creation you intend me to be.

Voice of the Aging Parent

At my age it's easy to feel out of sorts—even grumpy.
I can't see well; I can't hear well either.
I can't go places on my own, and I am not supposed to eat my
  favorite foods.
My joints ache, and I move slowly.
I have to take fifteen pills a day.
Growing old is not for sissies—whoever said that wasn't kidding.
Most days I make an effort not to dwell on these harsh realities.
I try to focus on the blessings of late life, but at times my mood
  gets low.
I start to feel unbalanced, like something's not right.
O Lord, when my threshold for frustration is nonexistent, fill me
  with your patience.
Show me a better way.
Reshape the clay, and make me into something new.
Something beautiful. Something useful.
So that I may serve others in your holy name.

Moving Forward Together

Meditate on the scripture reading from Ephesians and think about your life. What causes you to feel off-balance? What practice would help you center your life on God? What things in your life do you need to discard? How can you reprioritize your life so that you can better care for your most important relationships? Be creative in finding ways to center yourself on God. Create a playlist of worship songs that reinforce God's promises. Be faithful in keeping a prayer journal. Collect scripture verses that speak of God's truth in your life.

Prayer

You, O Lord, are the master potter, and I am the clay. Help me weigh my priorities on the scale of scripture and prayer. Then give me courage enough to trust you to mold me according to your plan. Amen.

CHANGE

Philippians 3:12-14

Not that I have already obtained this or have already reached the goal;
but I press on to make it my own, because Christ Jesus has made me his
own. Beloved, I do not consider that I have made it my own; but this
one thing I do: forgetting what lies behind and straining forward to
what lies ahead, I press on toward the goal for the prize of the heavenly
call of God in Christ Jesus.

Voice of the Adult Child

I wish that change wasn't so difficult for my aging mother.
She clings desperately to yesterday and won't let go.
She wears the same clothes and hairstyle.
She watches the same television reruns and listens to the same music.
Not long ago she would learn a new card game or try an
    unfamiliar food.
But no more.
She now finds safety and comfort in routine and repetition.
She refuses to learn how to use a computer and imagines all kinds
    of problems that might occur if she does.
I think she's convinced herself that she's not smart enough.
Not quick-witted enough.
She'd rather me do things for her than learn for herself.
Doesn't she realize that change comes whether she wants it or not?
She complains that she doesn't know what her grandchildren are
    talking about.
The truth is, she has no desire to learn about what interests them.
And so each new day becomes exactly like the last—monotonous
    and boring.
O Lord, how can I help her out of this deep rut?

Voice of the Aging Parent

O Lord, I am living in the midst of a storm.

Not just any storm—the perfect storm.

All the elements have come together to create a worst-case scenario.

Just as the world is speeding up, my mind and body are
    slowing down.

Never has change occrred as quickly as it is happening to me
    right now.

Dear God, you know I have experienced lots of change in my
    lifetime, but this change feels different.

The pace of technology makes it impossible for me to keep up.

By the time I master one gadget, it's already out-of-date.

I remember when a household had one telephone number;

the television had only a handful of channels.

We used encyclopedias and atlases to get our information.

Nowadays if you don't know how to use the latest technology, the
    world mocks you and makes you feel inferior.

Why should I even care about pop culture?

Every day I deal with change—losing home, independence, people I
    love, and a sense of purpose.

Even the little changes in life are enough to disorient me.

O Lord, I am weary of trying to walk on shifting sand.

Moving Forward Together

When life changes at a dizzying pace, you may be tempted to hunker down and wait for the storm to blow over. Life can seem unsettling and daunting. But being a disciple means growing, and growing means changing, pressing on. Even necessary change is hard, but learning how to embrace it is key to faithful aging.

Reflect on the scripture and think about how change is impacting your life right now. What fears are you harboring? Consider specific ways you can embrace change as a way to continue to grow as a disciple. Think of ways you can help family members deal with the frustrations of change.

Prayer

Change is hard, Lord, no matter my age. Forgive me when I get a whiff of change and refuse to budge from my comfort zone. Help me to trust you with my greatest fears. Give my patience and courage as I lean forward into life. Amen.

ABOUT THE AUTHOR

Missy Buchanan, a nationally recognized older adult advocate, has appeared on *Good Morning America* and several other television and radio shows. Missy is the author of *Living with Purpose in a Worn-Out Body, Talking with God in Old Age, Don't Write My Obituary Just Yet, Aging Faithfully, and Joy Boosters.* She coauthored *My Story, My Song: Mother-Daughter Reflections on Faith* with Lucimarian Roberts and Robin Roberts.

Missy Buchanan lives in Rockwall, Texas, with her husband, Barry. In addition to her busy writing and speaking schedule, Missy enjoys visiting older adult friends in three senior care centers weekly.

For more information, visit her website MissyBuchanan.com.

OTHER BOOKS FOR OLDER ADULTS AND THEIR LOVED ONES

10 Gospel Promises for Later Life
Jane Marie Thibault (978-0-8358-9801-0)

At the Edge of Life: Conversations When Death Is Near
Richard L. Morgan (978-0-8358-1332-7)

Fire in the Soul: A Prayer Book for Later Years
Richard L. Morgan (978-0-8358-0879-8)

*No Act of Love Is Ever Wasted: The Spirituality of Caring
for Persons with Dementia*
Jane Marie Thibault & Richard L. Morgan (978-0-8358-9995-6)

Not Alone: Encouragement for Caregivers
Nell E. Noonan (978-0-8358-9982-6)

Pilgrimage into the Last Third of Life: 7 Gateways to Spiritual Growth
Jane Marie Thibault & Richard L. Morgan (978-0-8358-1117-0)

Settling In: My First Year in a Retirement Community
Richard L. Morgan (978-0-8358-9908-6)

Shaping a Life of Significance for Retirement
R. Jack Hansen & Jerry P. Haas (978-0-8358-1025-8)

The Struggles of Caregiving: 28 Days of Prayer
Nell E. Noonan (978-0-8358-1091-3)

To order, call 1-800-972-0433 or visit bookstore.upperroom.org.

CPSIA information can be obtained at www.ICGtesting.com
Printed in the USA
LVOW01s0020201214

419661LV00012B/188/P